Her Red Wine Lore

Kristina Harris

BookLeaf Publishing
India | USA | UK

Presentation by *BookLeaf Publishing*

Web: www.bookleafpub.com

E-mail: info@bookleafpub.com

ISBN: 9789357446655

First edition 2022

DEDICATION

This book is dedicated to the four paws that saved a life, the black beauty, Bilbo.

ACKNOWLEDGEMENT

With thanks to my mother and sisters for putting up with my shit and forever worrying about me.
A big thank you to my best friends, who have been there through thick and thin.
And finally, the wine producers of this world.

Finally free.

Stretching, reaching for my dreams and goals,

doing it so while climbing out of dark holes.

Being so open and vulnerable, trying not to fear the unknown.

Pen to paper, scraps of sheet on the floor.

From reading this book, you're gonna know me some more.

To get things off my chest, take the lid off the bottle and set my hidden thoughts free.

Come on, take a ticket, ride this roller coaster of emotions, just you and me.

Hip hip hooray

This book is not intentionally going to be all
doom and gloom,
but some days are hard, and I struggle to make
the positivity bloom.

To have an outlet for my words, without getting
them twisted.
Makes me feel free and trust me I missed it.

Some days the words flow, and I cannot make
them stop,
I must get them all out before I go pop.
But some days I can't even make a single sound,
All I can hear is my heavy heartbeat pound.

THIS WAY UP

Clearing and cleaning out the debris,
of a future that is past.
No longer on the agenda,
as our love failed to last.

Packing up the boxes,
while sewing up my seams.
Wrapping newspaper and bubble wrap
around all my hopes and dreams.

Onwards I go.
Come what may.
Tomorrow is a new day.

Deafening

The silence is ringing in my ears,
I can't seem to focus straight while fighting back
the tears.

The lump in my throat slowly wants to dissipate,
While my grief slowly rises in hope to escape.

It's the same movie, but a different scene.
Slowly closing my eyes, hoping it's a dream.

DEAD

Cracked and broken,
my heart and my mind.
Too late to stop and
rewind the time.
The damage is done,
it's hit every nerve.

Denial is a bitch,
but she's yours now to keep.
I don't need her now,
I've given all I can weep.

Enjoy your freedom,
Don't mourn our love.
Because it's the break of day,
enough is enough.

Goodbye.
So long.
It's been quite a ride,
all the love that lingered,
has finally died.

Innocence

Oh, to be a child again,
So happy and free.
Running around a park,
or climbing a tree.

Scraped knees.
Grass stains.
Playing games.

Eating ice cream,
feeding a duck,
playing hide and seek,
getting covered in muck.

Fairytales

Once upon a time we were so happy.
However, things turned sour, and I had no
control or power.

How did it end up like this?
Where did it go wrong?
PUFF! and our relationship had gone.

You said you loved me,
As I did too.
But when push comes to shove,
it clearly wasn't enough.

So goodbye my solace
and the comfort of your hands,
But I'm off to search within truer lands.

Jameson

Ultimately there is no-one left to save you,
you have to save yourself.
It's a dog-eat-dog world, and every day we have
to compete.
You have to give yourself the biggest bark, or
end in defeat.

My love that I have had for you, has been the
greatest hardship that I've been through.
I've tirelessly loved you, day in, day out.
But now I'm left battered and blue.
You made me believe I was more than what I
really was to you.

You've used, abused and really left me confused.
I thought I meant more. I thought I felt your
love.
Yet here I am, crying on the floor.
You're a fucking selfish... and the times we had I
will always somehow adore.
But so long tainted love, I choose to no longer
endure.

Stars & Dust.

Hanging by a thread, my little bit of hope.
It's starting to fray, with all this shit,
I cannot cope.
I cannot cope.
Days are getting long; nights just turn to dust.
Slowly, soon, forget, my tears turn to rust.
My soul escaping out into the depths of the star
lit sky.
Farewell to it all, pleasure, pain and fear.
Don't be coming back, 'til I awaken sometime
next year.
To love again, my second chance, stars will fill
my eyes.
Goodbye old lover, a new one has arrived...

Old friend

All these things have become obviously bold.
You're looking so old.
Your eyes have grown tired, the light has
become dreary and cold.
Your get up and go has almost expired.
So sad and so glum,
lying and waiting,
waiting for the peace to come.
Fields of green, just to run and run.
A loyal companion is what you've always been.
Always by my side, keeping me company day
and night.
I love you dearly, my furry patch coloured
friend.
Thank you for staying with me until your bitter
end.

Wager

Bruised and abandoned,
lonely and blue,
All these things,
brought on by you.

A moment's lapse,
weak in the mind,
a web of lies slowly unbind.

I thought to myself,
this time it is true,
love conquers all,
except me and you.

Full of rage.
No signs of love,
from this we need to rise above.

Let's beat the odds,
dropkick the pain,
learn to smile once again.

Don't give up,
Don't let it win,
Let go of it all buried within.

Let's start a fresh,
Let us this time make it true,
all that should matter
is just me and you.

On the darkest of nights

I just live in this tree,
my lonely nest and me.
I built myself a home,
but it only inhabits me, all alone.

All alone, sometimes seems the best way to be.
No troubles, no cares, no stress, just me.
But when the wind blows,
I clutch on tight to this place I call home,
me, by myself, all alone.

I collect my twigs, my leaves and berries,
this is all I need just to be.
No troubles, no cares, no stress, except when the
wind blows.

My branches fuss and creak at night,
I toss and turn and try not to fright.
All alone, I pray by the moonlight night.
Don't blow me out, don't ruin me now.
Don't send me on my way.

I've given and taken so much,
please don't hurt me now or take it all away.
I've survived more and more each day.
From my ashes, I've made a home,
I've done this. I've done this all alone.

I'm better this way, I cause no-one harm, stress
or sadness.
Just leave me be, leave me alone along with my
rootless tree.

In your eyes, in my mind.

I feel like I'm the only one that's trying.
You don't seem to care.
While I'm left standing alone crying.
This emptiness is so hard to bear.

Why are you being so cold?
Should I give up this endless fight?
Give up, move on, is all I'm being told.
Get you out of my mind and out of sight.

I feel there's nothing I can do.
These feelings are out of sync.
I'm fed up with feeling these feelings for you.
You're dragging me down, killing my soul.

Fourteen

I thought I made peace with it,
several years ago.
But recently it's bubbled to the surface.
And now is the time to let it all go.

You were in the wrong.
Brainwashing a girl so young.
You got inside my head.
Messing up my thoughts and feelings,
I spent most of my teens wishing I was dead.

I wish it never happened,
I wish we never met.
You almost ruined my life.
But now is the time to forgive,
to heal,
and to truly forget.

Anxiety, my best friend.

When the clouds roll in and the storm roars on.
When the dark grips your hand with a force so
tight.
When the joy struggles to shower you in light.
You get caught off balance and lose track of
sight.
Gone is a life full of colour, each day becomes a
fight.
Remember nothing is fixed and the cracks will
fill up,
And sooner or later you will bare up.

Veterans

Old habits die hard.
We're both battled scarred.
Fights beyond repair,
as we slowly lost despair.

We're not destined to win this war.
I tried and every time I headed for the door.
It's just not meant to be.
Forever this endless love between you and me.

<3

Love is the word in which our heart is crying
out.
Love is a feeling that doesn't have doubt.
Love is an emotion that we can share freely.
Love can be something we can't always feel but
its presence is there.
Love is a mass amount of what you mean to me.

Love isn't a fortune; it can't always be told.
Your heart decides upon who is yours truly.
Love can be bold, but we can't always see.
Only one kiss can set it free.
Love is speechless, there are no words.
The day I met you I know a feeling could grow.

It can happen in a moment of time,
or even a year or two.
Love is forever within you.
Love knows its path.
At the end of the day,
your heart will always get its way.

Feels like Home

The smell of log fires,
And crisp Autumn in the air.
Takes me back to a place,
where I am free without a care.

Filled with warmth,
And sweet Autumn delight,
I feel home,
home on this chilly September night.

She's coming back

Surrounded by people who love me dearly.
Helping me back to me.
Getting me too see through my own eyes clearly.

To be myself, feels like coming home.
No longer hiding in a battle zone.
No more moaning or crying down the phone.

It took me a while to see the light,
I no longer want to fuss or fight.
I want a life of love and sweet delight.
And this time I want to keep it with all my
might.

Magnificent

To finally come out of the darkness
and into the light.
Into a love that holds my value
and gives me delight.

A love for me being me,
and what I need to be free.
Accepting, forgiving, understanding
and empowering me.

To hold that space,
that I need so dear.
Comfortably me,
without any fear.

Thank you for knowing me,
and accepting who I am,
for better or worse
and without a frown.

My deepest friend,
the one who knows my soul,
leading me always on to my goals.

Don't ever fear that you need to be free,
because standing by my side,
you will always be.

To live without limits,
to be who you are.
Exploring yourself,
no matter how far.

Only you can do what is right for you.
But I will be here,
to help and to understand. To love you right
back,
without any demand.

Let's just promise to never lose our glow.
Whatever happens between us,
only we need to know.

Haunted no more.

Longing for closure,
from all that has passed.
Excited to move on,
for my heart to be in peace at last.
Letting go of the ghosts,
No more heart-breaking screams.
Finally turning nightmares into dreams.
Opening and letting it all out.
Letting go of all the shit I keep thinking about.
I'm tired, I'm done, I no longer want to fight.
No more battling the demons in my head at
night.
I'm done.
Time to close this book and turn out the light.

www.ingramcontent.com/pod-product-compliance
Lightning Source LLC
Chambersburg PA
CBHW070729160726
48003CB00006BA/2422